BODY WORKS

MY MESSY BODY

LZA FROMER AND FRANCINE GERSTEIN MD

Illustrated by Joe Weissmann

TUNDRA BOOKS

Published in Canada by Tundra Books,
75 Sherbourne Street, Toronto, Ontario M5A 2P9

Published in the United States by Tundra Books of Northern New York,
P.O. Box 1030, Plattsburgh, New York 12901

Library of Congress Control Number: 2010940340

Library and Archives Canada Cataloguing in Publication

Fromer, Liza

My messy body / Liza Fromer and Francine Gerstein ; illustrated by Joe Weissmann.
(Body works)

ISBN 978-1-77049-202-8

1. Human body – Juvenile literature. 2. Human physiology – Juvenile
literature. 3. Human anatomy – Juvenile literature.
I. Gerstein, Francine II. Weissmann, Joe, 1947- III. Title.
IV. Series: Body works (Toronto, Ont.)

QP37.F764 2011   j612   C2010-907305-3

We acknowledge the financial support of the Government of Canada through the Book
Publishing Industry Development Program (BPIDP) and that of the Government of Ontario
through the Ontario Media Development Corporation's Ontario Book Initiative.
We further acknowledge the support of the Canada Council for the Arts and the Ontario
Arts Council for our publishing program.

ONTARIO ARTS COUNCIL
CONSEIL DES ARTS DE L'ONTARIO

Medium: watercolor on paper

Design: Leah Springate

Printed and bound in China

1 2 3 4 5 6   16 15 14 13 12 11

Also available in this Body Works series by Liza Fromer and Francine Gerstein MD, illustrated by Joe Weissmann

Authors' Note

The information in this book is to help you understand your body and learn why it works the way it does.

It's important that you see your family doctor at least once each year. If you're worried about your health or think you might be sick, speak to an adult and see your doctor.

Does it ever seem like there's always something dripping out of your body? From tears to sweat, earwax to snot, pee to poo, and, on a bad day, vomit to pus, your body can get pretty messy. Okay, it all sounds really gross, but your body is just doing its job, and sometimes that job can get yucky.

It's nothing to be embarrassed about because this is exactly how your body is supposed to work. Whether you're a movie star, a teacher, an astronaut, or a bus driver, everyone's body does the same jobs!

By the way. . .
When you see MT in this book, it stands for Medical Term.

TEARS

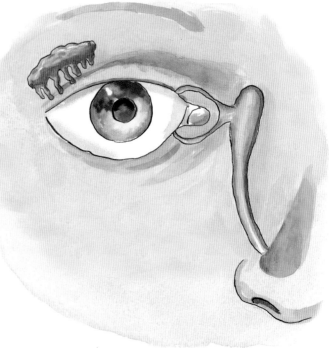

Tears are made of water, oil, and mucus. The watery part is produced by glands above your outer eyebrows; the oily part is produced by glands at the corners of your eyelids; and the mucus part comes from cells lining the inside of your eyelids.

When you blink, your eyelids spread your tears across the surface of your eyes, keeping them moist and clear of dust and other irritating particles. These irritating particles actually cause more tears to be produced. The tears go down tiny drains (MT: lacrimal puncta), through a narrow channel, and into a small container (MT: lacrimal sac). When you cry, there are too many tears for your special eye-drainage system to handle, so excess tears flow out of your eyes and down your cheeks.

The lacrimal sac is the upper part of a special duct that connects to the nasal passage, which is why your nose runs when you cry. Some people can even taste their tears as they drain from their nasal cavity into their throat. Think of tears as the cleaning fluid for your eyes. Just like the way windshield-wiper fluid sprays on the front window of your car, tears clean your eyeballs and your eyelids are the wipers.

#1 Onions contain sulfur, a gas that stimulates our tear-producing glands. That's why people cry when they cut into them!

#2 Newborn babies cry without tears. They are so young that their tear-making systems aren't ready to work yet.

True or False?

Humans are the only mammals that shed tears when they are sad. (*True.* If your dog is unhappy, he shows you in other ways, but tears aren't one of them.)

SWEAT

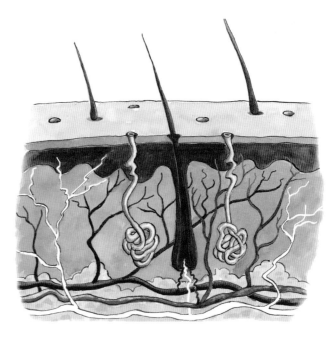

Your body creates heat when it's working properly. But sometimes it creates more heat than you can handle – when you exercise, when you're outside on a hot day, or when you're nervous. Your body makes sweat to get rid of that extra heat and to cool you down. In fact, you're constantly sweating, but you don't always feel it.

Sweat is made by your eccrine and apocrine glands (known as sweat glands), which live in your skin. Eccrine glands are all over your body, especially on the palms of your hands, the soles of your feet, and on your forehead. The sweat they produce contains water and salt. Apocrine glands are found mostly in your armpits and groin, but they don't start working until you're in your teens. These glands produce watery and salty sweat too, but this sweat also contains protein and fat. The average person has around 2.5 million sweat glands! With that many, you'd think you'd be soaking wet all the time.

Sweat glands have two parts: one part makes the sweat and the other acts as a path to the surface of the skin. When sweat is pushed to the surface, the water evaporates and turns into a gas (like steam rising from a kettle), leaving the salt, protein, and fat behind on your skin. This is why your skin tastes salty when you sweat.

On its own, sweat doesn't have an odor. But when bacteria eat (MT: metabolize) the protein and fat left behind on your skin, they produce a smell. Luckily, the smelly sweat is found just in the areas of your body that have apocrine glands. This is the reason why you need to use deodorant only on your underarms.

#1 Lips don't have sweat glands.

#2 Many animals can't sweat because they don't have sweat glands. Dogs, for example, pant and hang out their tongues to get rid of excess body heat.

Doctor says:

"When you sweat, you lose a lot of salt and water from your body, and that can dehydrate you. It's important to drink more liquids when you exercise and when you're outside in hot weather."

EARWAX

Earwax (MT: cerumen) is something you usually want to clean out of your ears, but the truth is, it's there to keep your ears clean. Earwax cleans, moistens, and protects your ears from bugs, dirt, and dust. By doing so, it prevents dry, itchy ears and infections.

Earwax is made by glands in the ear canal. And although everyone has it, earwax doesn't always look the same. It can be dry, flaky, and light-colored or wet and brown-colored.

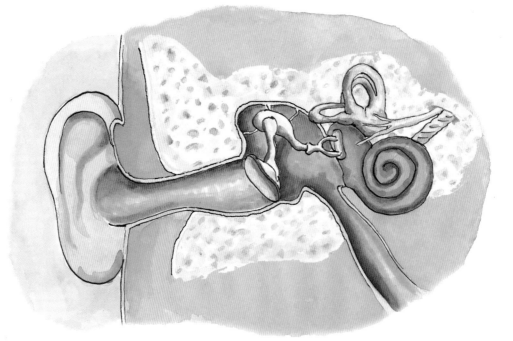

You might be surprised to hear that you shouldn't put anything in your ears, not even a cotton swab, because it could get stuck, poke a hole in your eardrum, or damage your ear canal. Ears are amazing self-cleaning machines! Skin in the ear canal grows outwards, from the eardrum to the outside of the ear. Although you don't feel it, that skin continually grows, moving the earwax and its special antibodies that fight infections out of your ears.

Some people's ears make too much wax, which can make it hard for them to hear. If that happens to you, see your doctor, who will clean them out.

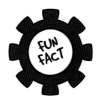 **A cough can sometimes be caused by earwax pressing on your ear canal.**

Doctor says:
"You wouldn't believe what I've pulled out of people's ears: cotton-swab tips, beads, even fake plant parts. Don't put *anything* in your ears!"

True or False?
Most candles in North America contain up to 5% human earwax. *(False and gross!)*

SNOT

Snot (MT: nasal mucus) is mucus that lines the inside of the nostrils. It's made up mostly of water, with some salt, proteins, carbohydrates, and nostril cells. Some of the proteins are called antibodies because they help you fight off viruses and bacteria (also called germs or bugs) that could make you sick.

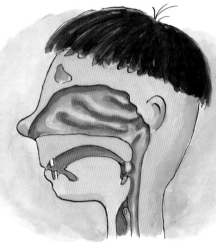

Since snot is sticky, it traps particles of dust and dirt. When you sneeze or blow your nose, some of those particles go flying out! You swallow what doesn't come out of your nose (gross!) because it drips down the back of your throat. But, this time, you don't have to worry about the germs that come along with it because the acid in your stomach gets rid of them. Any snot left over in your nose dries and hardens to become boogers.

Your nose makes more snot when you're sick or when something irritates your nostrils, such as dust. This is why more mucus drips from your nose when you have a cold or are in a dusty room. Everyone needs snot in their nose because it acts like a filter to protect their lungs from bugs and other particles.

FUN FACTS

#1 Snot is actually clear. The stuff that is stuck in it gives it a green color.

#2 The speed of a sneeze is over 90 miles (145 kilometers) per hour.

#3 Cold and flu viruses can live on surfaces from a few seconds to two days, depending on the virus and the surface. Flu viruses stay around longer than cold viruses and live longer on smooth surfaces (like doorknobs) than on fabrics (like clothing).

Doctor says:

"You shouldn't pick your nose. It looks gross, and you can spread germs by using that finger to touch objects that other people are likely to use. Also, if you pick your nose too hard, you can get a nosebleed."

PEE

It's no surprise that if you drink a lot of liquids, you'll probably have to pee (MT: urinate) – hope you didn't just put on your snow pants! But did you know that a lot of your pee comes from the solid food you eat? Although it's called solid, food is mostly water, especially fruits and veggies. An apple, for example, is made up of 80% water.

Your body is made up of 50 to 70% water. When you drink or eat, the liquid or food travels down the esophagus into the stomach and then to the intestines, where all the nutrients and water are absorbed through the walls of the digestive tract and into your bloodstream.

Once the water gets into your bloodstream, it's used for lots of different jobs, including making snot, tears, sweat, and the other drippy things you're learning about right now. Whatever liquid is left over heads to your kidneys, which are your body's cleaning machines. They send nutrients back to your body and filter out the waste. The waste is what we call pee.

Each person has two kidneys. The pee travels from the kidneys, down tubes (MT: ureters), and into the bladder, which is a pee-holding tank. When your tank is full, you're ready to pee. Your brain tells your bladder to relax, and the urine goes down your urethra and out of your body.

#1 A person cannot live without water for more than a few days.

#2 Some people are born with only one kidney, known as a "horseshoe kidney."

Doctor says:

"If you have to pee, you shouldn't hold it in for very long because this could lead to a bladder infection."

"Your pee changes color throughout the day because of the concentration. Usually it's darker in the morning and lighter later on because of all the drinks you've had, which dilute your pee."

POO

Isn't it strange that the yummy food you eat turns into yucky, smelly poo (MT: feces)? Well, here's why …

After you chew your food and swallow, it goes down the esophagus and into your stomach. Your stomach twists and churns, mixing up the chewed food with digestive juices. But that is just the start of the journey. The next stop is the small intestine. Once the food gets there, it's broken down into tiny components called nutrients, which your body uses in different ways. Fats from foods such as chocolate and avocados turn into fatty acids. Proteins from foods like meat and fish break down into amino acids. Starches from foods like bread and cereal turn into sugar or glucose.

Tiny blood vessels absorb these nutrients and carry them to all the cells in your body. The unabsorbed leftovers go into the large intestine (MT: colon), where water and salt are absorbed back into your bloodstream. The *leftover* leftovers are the waste, which is what we call poo.

 **#1 Poo is made up of approximately 75% water.**

#2 Cow and horse poo are sometimes used for fertilizer because they are rich in nutrients, which help plants grow.

Doctor says:

 "If your poo is watery and comes out quickly, you have diarrhea. There are many causes of diarrhea, including the stomach flu. If your poo is hard to push out, you have constipation. You can become constipated if you don't drink enough water or eat enough fiber (found in fruits, veggies, and wholegrain bread)."

VOMIT

When you vomit, your tummy muscles (MT: abdominal muscles) contract and push down very hard on your stomach. This moves whatever is in your stomach up and out through your mouth.

Vomiting is a symptom of many different problems. For example, some children vomit when they have a fever or an ear infection. Vomiting also gets rid of stuff in your stomach that is not healthy to eat or drink. If you eat food that is spoiled, you might not realize it, but your body does. Vomiting is a very important clue that there is something wrong and you should find out what it is!

#1 Vomit has many nicknames: puke, throw up, hurl, yak, and barf.

#2 Some pregnant women get morning sickness, which makes them feel like vomiting.

True or False?

Some people get motion sickness and may vomit when they are traveling by boat, plane, or car. (*True.* And any bumps or waves along the way will probably make it worse.)

PUS

Pus (MT: purulent discharge) can form in different parts of your body – sometimes you see it and sometimes you don't. Pus is a signal that your body is fighting off an infection caused by bacteria. But the pus isn't what does the fighting. The real heroes are the infection-fighting cells (MT: white blood cells), which can be seen only under a microscope. Pus is what's left over after those cells fight to make you better.

You might have seen pus if you've ever had a pimple. It probably looked white, but it can show up in a rainbow of colors. Sometimes it even has a stinky smell.

Doctor says:

"If you see pus coming from your body, don't ignore it. Tell an adult and see your doctor to find out the cause."

Isn't it amazing what your messy body can do!

Glossary

Carbohydrates, cell, dehydration, digestive tract, duct, glands, glucose, mucus, protein, virus.

Carbohydrates: One of the main energy sources for the body. They are mostly sugars and starches that come from foods like pasta, bread, and cereal.

Cell: Often called the building block of life because it is the smallest unit that can still be called a living thing.

Dehydration: A state where the body doesn't have enough fluids. It happens when more water is going out of your body than is being taken in.

Digestive tract: A very long pathway that goes from your mouth to your anus, including your esophagus, stomach, and intestines.

Duct: A tube that things like tears can pass through.

Glands: Produce what is needed for certain body functions. For example, there is a gland that makes a hormone that tells your body to grow.

Glucose: A very tiny form of sugar that provides energy to the body's cells.

Mucus: A slippery substance that lubricates and protects different parts of the body.

Protein: One of the three energy sources for the body (the other two are carbohydrates and fat).

Virus: A microscopic infectious agent that can only replicate in a living cell.